funk it up

To Mum, Dad and Marc

THIS IS A CARLTON BOOK

Text, design and special photography copyright
© 2001 Carlton Books Limited

This edition published by Carlton Books Limited 2002
20 Mortimer Street, London W1T 3JW

A CIP catalogue record for this book is available from
the British Library
ISBN 1 84222 640 1

Printed and bound in Italy

Editorial Manager: Venetia Penfold
Art Director: Penny Stock
Senior Art Editor: Barbara Zuñiga
Executive Editor: Zia Mattocks
Writer/Editor: Lisa Dyer
Designer: Nigel Soper
Photographer: Lucy Pope
Stylists: Petra Boase and Jane McAllister
Production Controller: Janette Burgin

Neither the authors nor the publisher can accept responsibility
for any accident, injury or damage that results from using the
ideas, information or advice offered in this book.

funk it up

customize your clothes and decorate your accessories
with paint, dye, bleach and transfers

Petra Boase

CARLTON
BOOKS

Contents

Printing & Painting

Exciting new products, from washable glitters and foils to puffa paints and stamp inks, make printing and painting on fabric both fun and inventive. Transfer prints enable a photograph to be copied on to T-shirts, and you can buy screen-printing equipment for creating your own designs. Whether you prefer stencilling or freehand design, the projects here will give you the opportunity to experiment.

Blue Star

THIS STAR AND GEMSTONE TOP invokes the spirited casual dressing of today's teen pop stars – all you need is bleached jeans, a diamanté belt and some killer boots to mimic their laid-back street-savvy style. You can either buy a star stencil from a home-decorating shop, or draw and cut one yourself.

HOW TO DO IT

1 Cover a flat work surface with newspaper. Place the vest (tank) top on the work surface and insert a piece of cardboard measuring the width and length of the top to separate back and front.

2 If you are cutting your own stencil, draw a star on to the stencil card. Alternatively, trace a star from a book or magazine on to tracing paper with pencil, tape the tracing paper, lead side down, on to the stencil card and retrace over it to transfer the image. Place the stencil card on a cutting mat and cut out the stencil with a craft knife (see page 72).

3 Position the stencil on the centre front of the top, about 10 cm (4 in) from the neckline. Measure to ensure it is centred and straight, then secure it in place with masking tape.

4 Dab the stencil brush into blue fabric paint and apply the paint to the top through the cut-out star (see page 72). Do not overload the brush, or paint will seep underneath the stencil. Reapply the paint, as necessary. When you have finished, remove the tape and carefully lift off the stencil. Wash the stencil brush immediately.

5 Along the neckline and between the straps, use a fabric marker to mark the points where you want to position the diamantés. Dab a small amount of fabric glue on to one mark at a time and stick on the diamantés, using the tweezers (see page 73).

6 Leave the top on the flat work surface for a few hours until the glue has hardened and the paint has dried. Follow the fabric paint manufacturer's instructions to fix the paint, usually by ironing on to the reverse side of the design.

WHAT YOU NEED

- Newspaper
- Grey cotton vest (tank top)
- Cardboard
- Stencil card, tracing paper, pencil or pen, cutting mat and craft knife, or a pre-cut star stencil
- Tape measure or ruler
- Masking tape
- Stencil brush
- Blue fabric paint
- Chalk or pen fabric marker
- Strong fabric glue
- 11 small silver flat-backed diamantés
- Tweezers
- Iron and ironing board

The Way of the East

ALTHOUGH THERE ARE A PLETHORA of printed tops for sale, if you have a favourite image you want on a T-shirt, you can easily make your own. Asian figures and motifs give an Eastern-inspired edge to clothing, inviting romantic images of far-off destinations. Whether you are interested in yoga, Buddhism or the *I Ching*, or just like the stylized images of Eastern art, source an image that you respond to. Try Buddha, Siva or just a quaint little Chinese figure like the one here, emblazoned across your chest.

WHAT YOU NEED
· Colour photocopy of a copyright-free Chinese character
· Scissors
· White T-shirt
· Tape measure or ruler

HOW TO DO IT

1 Take a colour photocopy of the Chinese character to a copy shop or T-shirt-printing shop that offers colour transfers on to T-shirts. Ask for the design to be photocopied on to transfer paper.

2 Cut out the design and take it back to the copy or printing shop with the long-sleeve white T-shirt. Centre the image on the front of the T-shirt, measuring to ensure that it is straight and centred. Ask for the design to be printed as positioned.

Line by Line

A PLAIN WHITE VEST (tank) top is printed with an abstract pattern of cut-out lines in a neon palette of colours inspired by modern art. Let screen-printing bring out the art student in you and research the work of Mondrian and other key figures in abstract or pop art to inspire striking designs.

WHAT YOU NEED

- Newspaper or an old sheet or fabric remnant
- Masking tape
- White vest (tank) top
- Cardboard
- Plain paper
- Scissors
- Screen-printing screen
- Turquoise, yellow and pink screen-printing inks
- Squeegee or long piece of cardboard

Tip

You could also use the technique to create horizontal and vertical stripes in various widths, or cut out notches along the length of newspaper to make irregular shapes or sawtoothed lines.

HOW TO DO IT

1 Cover a flat work surface with newspaper or an old sheet, securing it with masking tape. Place the top, front facing up, on the surface. Insert a piece of cardboard inside the top to separate back and front.

2 Arrange pieces of plain paper on top to create lines of varying widths for the first colour; here three lines were created for the turquoise ink. Make sure the top is exposed only in the areas you want coloured as lines – the rest of the top should be covered up with plain paper.

3 Place the screen over the top, taking care not to move the paper. Following the manufacturer's instructions, pour the first colour of ink (here turquoise) in a line along the top end of the screen.

4 Using the squeegee or a piece of cardboard, and holding the screen down firmly with one hand, scrape the ink from end to end to print the lines on to the top, using an even, firm action. Dab the squeegee or cardboard to remove excess ink, and repeat to print over the top twice (see page 71). Carefully remove the screen and the paper. Discard the paper and immediately wash the screen and squeegee. Allow the ink to dry for the recommended time.

5 When it is dry, repeat steps 2 to 4 to make the yellow line, allowing the line to overlap on to the blue. Use fresh paper, the cleaned screen, and either the cleaned squeegee or a new piece of cardboard for each colour. Repeat the technique to make the pink line. You can make as many lines in as many colours as you like.

6 Wash the screen and the squeegee, and leave the top flat to dry for the recommended time. When the paint is dry, fix the printed design, if necessary, according to the screen-printing instructions.

Stamp-printed
Flowers

STAMP PRINTING IS ONE OF THE EASIEST, and one of the earliest, methods of decorating textiles. Here a floral repeat motif is stamped on to a bright lime fluoro top, creating images that are uniform and highly intricate in design. The ink shades in outlines and certain areas, leaving other areas for the background to show through. Stamps in a glorious variety of forms can be bought from home-decorating shops or department stores.

WHAT YOU NEED

· Lime cotton vest (tank) top
· Cardboard
· 'Invisible' or 'fade-away' pen
  fabric marker (optional)
· Tape measure or ruler
· Fabric stamping ink or paint
· Roller
· Flower rubber stamp
· Plain paper
· Iron and ironing board

HOW TO DO IT

1 Place the top on a flat work surface and insert a piece of cardboard, measuring the width and length of the top, inside the top to separate back and front.

2 Here six flowers were stamped on randomly. If you prefer to work out placement first, measure and mark the central positions for the flowers with a small dot, using the fabric marker.

3 Roll the roller in the fabric-stamping ink or paint, then roll the paint on to the surface of the stamp (see page 71).

4 Press the stamp on to the T-shirt and hold it down firmly so that all the details of the stamp print on the fabric. Practise first by stamping on to plain white paper. Gently and carefully lift off the stamp.

5 Reapply the ink or paint and repeat steps 3 and 4 to print the other flowers. Leave to dry. Wash the stamp and roller immediately.

6 When the paint is dry, follow the fabric paint manufacturer's instructions to fix the paint; usually this entails ironing on to the reverse side of the design.

Rainbow Stripes

Hand-painted rainbow lines give a new slant to trendy stripes. The bold irregular stripes have an artistic dripping quality that creates movement, rather than static linearity, in the design. You could also work just one or two horizontal or diagonal stripes across the vertical lines to create intersecting planes for added visual interest.

WHAT YOU NEED

- Newspaper
- White T-shirt
- Cardboard
- Plain, non-shiny, paper
- Scissors
- Fabric paints with fine nozzles in assorted colours (here 9 colours were used)
- Iron and ironing board

HOW TO DO IT

1 Cover a flat work surface with newspaper and place the T-shirt on it, front facing up. Insert a piece of card, the length of the shirt, to separate back and front.

2 Cut strips of plain paper to measure the length of the shirt. You will need a strip for each painted line.

3 Using one colour of fabric paint, squeeze a line of paint vertically down one long side of the T-shirt, along an outside edge. Lay a strip of paper over the paint, smooth it down with your hand and then carefully lift off the paper. Discard the paper.

4 Repeat step 3 to make stripes in different colours, allowing a gap of approximately 5 cm (2 in) between each one. Take care to use thin strips of paper and work carefully (from right to left if you are right-handed) so that previously painted stripes are not smudged.

5 Leave the T-shirt on the flat work surface to dry. Follow the fabric paint manufacturer's instructions to fix the paint; usually this entails ironing on to the reverse side of the design.

Silver-foil '30'

SILVER METALLIC FOIL creates a flash of high-shine against a bright teal-blue background. Make this your all-time most lucky shirt by using your personal lucky number. The effect can be created on tiny cropped T-shirts, vests or slinkier tops for a roller-girl from *Boogie Nights* look.

WHAT YOU NEED

- Teal-blue T-shirt
- Cardboard
- Tracing paper and pencil
- Stencil card
- Cutting mat
- Craft knife
- Masking tape
- Tape measure or ruler
- Stencil brush
- Transfer-foil glue
- Silver transfer foil
- Plain paper
- Iron and ironing board

HOW TO DO IT

1 Place the T-shirt on a flat work surface. Insert a piece of cardboard inside the shirt to separate back and front.

2 Source numbers from a design book, use a computer font or photocopy numbers you see in a magazine or book and enlarge them to the required size. Here each number measures 15 x 10 cm (6 x 4 in). Trace the outline of the numbers on to tracing paper with a pencil, making sure there is enough space between the numbers. Tape the tracing paper, lead side down, on to the stencil card and retrace over it to transfer the image. Place the stencil card on a cutting mat and cut out the numbers with a craft knife (see page 72). Turn the stencil card over so that the numbers read right side up.

3 Position the stencil on the centre front of the T-shirt. Measure to ensure that the stencil is centred and straight and secure it at each corner with masking tape.

4 Using the stencil brush, dab the glue evenly inside the cut-outs of the stencil. Remove the masking tape and lift off the stencil. Leave the glue to dry until it becomes clear; usually this takes four to eight hours.

5 Place the silver transfer foil, foil side up, over the glue and smooth down. Fix the foil in place by placing plain paper over the foil and pressing with a hot iron (see page 70). Remove the paper to reveal the design.

Purple-foil Heart

MAKE AN IMPACT with a simple larger-than-life graphic shape. If a heart doesn't inspire you, try a diamond, flower or star. Foil transfer leaf enables you to mimic the metallic detailing seen on so many shop-bought tops. The foil is worked in a similar way to gilding, with the foil pressed over glue.

Tip
For an extra-glittery effect, glue gemstones or apply a thin line of glitter fabric paint around the outline of the shape (see pages 73 and 70).

WHAT YOU NEED
- Deep purple T-shirt
- Cardboard
- Stencil card
- Pencil or pen
- Cutting mat
- Craft knife
- Masking tape
- Tape measure or ruler
- Stencil brush
- Transfer foil glue
- Purple transfer foil
- Plain paper
- Iron and ironing board

HOW TO DO IT

1 Place the T-shirt, front facing up, on a flat work surface. Insert a piece of cardboard inside the T-shirt to separate back and front.

2 Cut out a heart stencil. Draw a heart measuring approximately 19 x 22 cm (7½ x 8½ in) on to the stencil card. Alternatively, cut out a paper heart and trace around it on to the stencil card. Cut out the heart stencil using a craft knife and cutting mat (see page 72).

3 Position the stencil on the centre front of the T-shirt. Measure to ensure that the stencil is centred and straight. Secure it at each corner with masking tape.

4 Using the stencil brush, dab the glue over the heart area. Remove the tape and lift off the stencil. Leave the glue to dry for four to eight hours until it is clear.

5 Following the manufacturer's instructions, place the purple transfer foil over the glue and smooth down. Fix the foil by placing plain paper over the foil and pressing with a hot iron (see page 70). Remove the paper.

Purple Dalmatian Spots

W HO LET THE DOGS OUT? Four different sizes of spots are used to create a lively all-over pattern that suggests a Dalmatian's coat. Try black spots on a white background for an authentic look, or go wild and work with multicoloured ink. Team it with jeans for a relaxed but fun look. The technique would work to good effect on skirts, bags, jackets or even on jeans – perhaps placing the spots randomly on the top half and back pockets of beaten-up distressed jeans.

WHAT YOU NEED

- Newspaper
- Lilac cotton T-shirt
- Cardboard
- Compasses and a pen
- 4 pieces of stencil card
- Cutting mat
- Craft knife
- 'Invisible' or 'fade-away' pen fabric marker (optional)
- Stencil brush
- Purple fabric paint
- Iron and ironing board

HOW TO DO IT

1 Cover a flat work surface with newspaper. Place the T-shirt on the work surface and insert a piece of cardboard to separate back and front.

2 Make stencils for four different-sized spots. Using compasses and a pen, draw each spot on to a separate piece of stencil card (see page 72). Place the cards on a cutting mat and cut out the circles with a craft knife.

3 The spots are randomly placed by working the larger ones first and filling in the empty areas with smaller spots. If you prefer to work out placement first, measure and mark the central positions for the spots with a small dot, using the fabric marker.

4 Position the largest stencil on the T-shirt in the desired position, making sure that the top is smooth and straight. Holding the stencil firmly in place around the edges with one hand, dab the stencil brush in purple fabric paint with your other hand. Apply the paint to the T-shirt through the cut-out circle (see page 72). Do not overload the brush, or paint will seep underneath the stencil. Reapply the paint to the brush, as necessary. When you have painted all of the circle, carefully lift off the stencil.

5 Repeat to paint on the other spots, continuing down in size from largest to smallest. If the stencil card will overlap on to previously painted spots, allow the paint to dry on those spots before beginning again. Wash the stencil brush and stencil cards, if reusing them, immediately.

6 Leave the T-shirt to dry. When the paint is completely dry, follow the fabric paint manufacturer's instructions to fix the paint; usually this entails ironing on the reverse side of the design.

Japanese
Blossom

A SINGLE, GRACEFUL STEM of cherry blossom arches across a pistachio-green skirt, creating a tranquil Eastern air. Keep the look subtle and don't overpower this delicate design with a cacophony of florals or prints. Simply team it with a subtle pink or white T-shirt and flat sandals.

WHAT YOU NEED

- Newspaper
- Masking tape
- Mint-green skirt (or one in another pastel colour, such as pale blue)
- Cardboard
- 'Invisible' or 'fade-away' pen fabric marker
- Fine- and medium-tipped artists' brushes
- Black, pale pink and rose-pink fabric paints
- Iron and ironing board

HOW TO DO IT

1 Cover a flat work surface with newspaper, securing it with tape. Decide whether you want the design on the front or back of the skirt, then place it on the work surface. Insert a piece of cardboard inside the skirt to separate back and front, then tape the skirt to the work surface so that the area you are going to paint is smooth and taut.

2 Draw the blossom branch freehand on to the skirt with the fabric marker. Sketch out the gently tapering branches first, and then add the blossoms on the highest branches.

3 Paint the design using the medium-tipped brush for filling in colour and the fine-tipped brush for adding detail. Paint the branch of the blossom first, using black fabric paint. Allow the paint to dry and wash the brush.

4 When the branch is dry, paint the blossom flowers and buds in a pale pink. Add darker rose-pink highlights to the blossoms, softly blending into the wet, pale pink colour at the edges. Wash the brushes immediately.

5 Leave the skirt on the flat work surface to dry. Follow the fabric paint manufacturer's instructions to fix the paint; usually this entails ironing on to the reverse side of the design.

Puffa Paint Spots

DECORATE A STRETCHY TOP with spots for an elegant and pretty look. An entirely novel way with spots, these embossed puffs give added texture and detail to a top. Concentrating more spots at the top and spacing them out gradually toward the bottom creates a starry effect, but you could also work them in rows or along seams.

WHAT YOU NEED

- Sleeveless cotton top
- Cardboard
- Tape measure
- Pink puffa paint with a fine nozzle
- Iron and ironing board

Tip

Try multicoloured dots on white for a more playful approach or work them on a satin bomber jacket for a groovier vibe.

HOW TO DO IT

1 Place the top, front facing up, on a flat work surface. Insert a piece of cardboard measuring the width and length of the top to separate back and front.

2 Squeeze small spots out of the tube of puffa paint on to the top. The harder you squeeze, the bigger the spot will be (practise on plain paper first). Here more spots were placed randomly near the top, with spots gradually dispersing toward the bottom.

3 When you have finished the design, leave the top flat overnight for the paint to dry.

4 When the paint is completely dry, turn the top inside out and slip it over the end of the ironing board. Iron the front of the top where the spots have been applied. Following the manufacturer's instructions, press the iron down carefully over the spots; do not glide the iron back and forth. The heat will make the painted spots puff up magically.

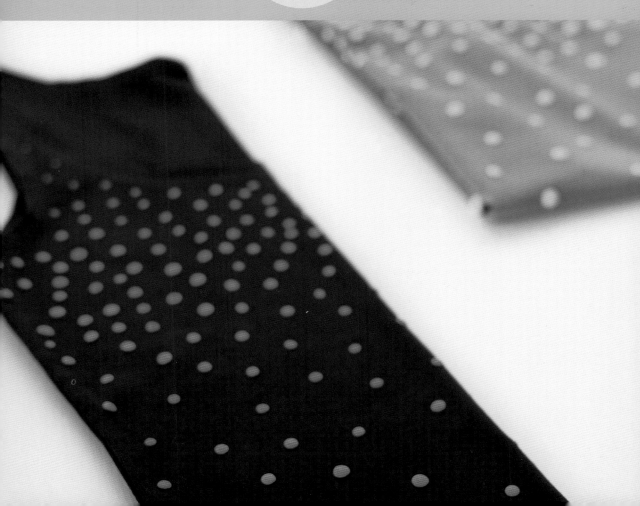

Red Leopard

DYING TO MIX WITH the JET SET? Au sauvage! Get yourself some leopard spots and you'll look the part, whether you are rubbing shoulders with the fashion pack or just aspiring to. Team these vibrant oh-so-hot orange spots with black leather trousers and a studded belt and blend in with the celeb crowd. For a more casual look, use the top to spice up military wear.

HOW TO DO IT

1 Cover a flat work surface with newspaper. Place the top on the work surface and insert a piece of cardboard to separate back and front.

2 Make sure that the top is smooth and straight, then position the leopard-print stencil on top and secure it to the work surface at each corner with masking tape.

3 Dab the stencil brush in red fabric paint and apply it to the top through the cut-out sections (see page 72). Hold down the edges of the stencil with your other hand if they begin to curl up; this will help to keep the edges crisp. Do not overload the brush, or paint will seep underneath the stencil. Reapply the red fabric paint to the brush, as necessary.

4 When you have painted through the entire stencil, remove the masking tape at the corners and carefully lift off the stencil. Leave the top to dry. Wash the stencil brush and stencil card, if reusing, immediately.

5 When the front is dry, you can stencil the back of the top, if desired. Simply repeat the steps above.

6 When the paint is completely dry, follow the fabric paint manufacturer's instructions to fix the paint; usually this entails ironing on the wrong side of the design.

WHAT YOU NEED

- Newspaper
- Orange vest (tank) top
- Cardboard
- Pre-cut leopard-print stencil (see Resources, page 79)
- Masking tape
- Stencil brush
- Red fabric paint
- Iron and ironing board

Big Pink Spot

WHAT YOU NEED

- Newspaper or an old sheet or fabric remnant
- Masking tape
- Orange cotton sweater
- Cardboard
- Plain paper
- Compasses, pen and scissors
- Tape measure or ruler
- Screen-printing screen
- Pink water-based screen-printing ink
- Squeegee or long piece of cardboard

A BRIGHT POP-ART SPOT makes a funky fashion statement, and the graphic simplicity of the design gives the sweater a unisex character. But remember that if you are working on a coloured background, the ink colour may not be pure – avoid green on orange, for example, if you don't want to get a murky brown colour.

HOW TO DO IT

1 Cover a flat work surface with newspaper or an old sheet, securing it to the surface with masking tape. Place the sweater, front facing up, on top. Insert a piece of cardboard inside to separate back and front.

2 Draw a large circle on a piece of plain paper, using the compasses and a pen. Here the circle is 22 cm (8½ in) in diameter. Cut it out to make a stencil (see page 72).

3 Position the paper stencil centrally on the front of the sweater. Make sure that the sweater is smoothed flat, then measure to make sure that the stencil is centred and straight. Secure it in place at each corner with masking tape. The rest of the sweater should be covered with newspaper. Place the screen on top.

4 Following the screen-printing instructions, pour the pink printing ink in a line longer than the width of the circle along the top end of the screen.

5 Using the squeegee or a piece of cardboard, and holding the screen down firmly with one hand, carefully scrape the ink from end to end to print the spot on the sweater, using an even, firm action. Dab the squeegee or cardboard to remove any excess ink, then repeat to print over the sweater twice (see page 71).

6 Carefully remove the screen and the paper. Discard the paper and immediately wash the screen and squeegee. Allow the ink to dry for the recommended time. When it is dry, fix the printed design according to the screen-printing instructions.

Winged 'PETRA' Shirt

IF YOU'D RATHER PLAY RUGBY than teeter around in stilettos, try the tomboy trend. A sporty top with your name on it can be paired with jeans for a relaxed weekend outfit. If you like the style, but are a true girl at heart, create the letters on a tiny T-shirt and wear with a pretty designer skirt for a street-cool meets haute-couture look.

WHAT YOU NEED

- Photocopies of letters
- Felt-tip pens
- Scissors
- Plain paper
- Orange T-shirt
- Tape measure or ruler

HOW TO DO IT

1 The letters here were designed using computer software and were printed out in colour, but you can take black-and-white photocopies of copyright-free typography and colour the letters, using felt-tip pens.

2 Cut out the letters. Place a piece of paper on the shirt and arrange the letters in a slightly curved formation. Measure to ensure the letters are straight and equally spaced. The first and last letters should be at the same level, and at the same distance from the side seams. Make a colour copy of the paper with the letters in place.

3 Take the photocopy to a copy shop or T-shirt printer that offers colour transfers on fabric and have the image printed directly on to the front of the T-shirt.

Alarm-clock Shirt

FOR ALL THOSE DESIGN JUNKIES out there, imprint an image of your favourite piece of technology on to your sweatshirt. This digital alarm clock may be just the type of design you love, or try a state-of-the-art image like a computer mouse or mobile (cell) phone, or go for nostalgic retro designs, such as an old-fashioned dial telephone.

WHAT YOU NEED

- Copyright-free image of an alarm clock or other gadget
- Pink felt-tip pen
- Grey sweatshirt

HOW TO DO IT

1 Using a copyright-free design, make a black-and-white photocopy of a picture of an alarm clock. Colour in the figures with a pink felt-tip pen to resemble the fluorescent read-out of a digital clock.

2 Take the photocopy to a copy shop or T-shirt-printing shop that offers colour transfers on fabric. Ask for the image to be transfer printed directly on to the front of the sweatshirt.

Cat & Dog
T-shirts

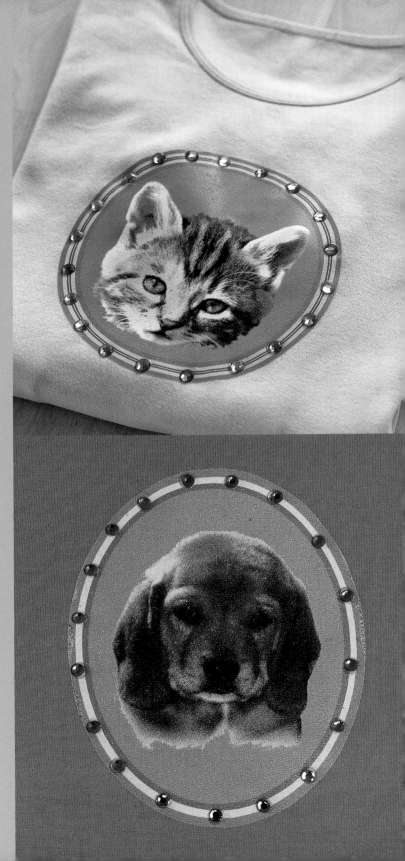

KEEP YOUR LOOK CUTE and kitsch with these T-shirts, which would also make a great gift. Pay homage to a well-loved pet by featuring your own dog or cat on the shirt. You can use a single colour, assorted colours or two alternating colours of gemstones to frame your animal picture.

WHAT YOU NEED

- Photocopy of your cat or dog (or any other animal)
- Scissors
- Coloured T-shirt
- Chalk or pen fabric marker
- Strong fabric glue
- 18 flat-backed gemstones in colours of your choice
- Tweezers

HOW TO DO IT

1 Make a colour photocopy of a cat or dog on a coloured background. Alternatively, if you have a computer and a scanner, scan a photograph of your pet into your computer and use your software to create a background frame for the image, before printing out the image from a colour printer. Take your image to a copy shop or T-shirt-printing shop that offers colour transfers. Ask for the image to be transfer printed directly on to the front of the T-shirt. Some photograph developers can even transfer print images taken from your own photographs on to T-shirts.

2 Place the printed T-shirt, front facing up, on a flat work surface. With the fabric marker, mark equally spaced positions for the gemstones around the frame of the design. Working one gemstone at a time, place a dab of glue on a marked position and carefully stick a gemstone in place using tweezers (see page 73). Leave the T-shirt flat until the glue is dry.

Glitter Flower

THE OUTLINE of a gigantic flowerhead, depicted in glitter and standing out in sharp relief from a dark background, makes a dramatic statement. Use a stylized profile of a just-opening bloom and work the design in the bottom corner of a T-shirt, with the stamens spraying outward. The glitter flower adds feminine appeal to an army-green T-shirt. Combine it with camouflage trousers and wear your hair in a rockabilly quiff (coif) for that happening butch look.

WHAT YOU NEED

- Newspapers
- Olive-green sleeveless cotton T-shirt
- Cardboard
- Masking tape
- 'Invisible' or 'fade-away' pen fabric marker
- Strong fabric glue with a thin nozzle
- Fine washable pink glitter

HOW TO DO IT

1 Cover a flat work surface with newspaper. Place the T-shirt on the work surface and insert a piece of cardboard to separate back and front. Secure the T-shirt to the work surface with masking tape around the edges of the cardboard so that the T-shirt's surface is smooth and taut.

2 Draw the design of the flower freehand on to the front of the T-shirt with the fabric marker. Here the design was inspired by an image from a flower book.

3 Practise squeezing out the fabric glue before you start; apply consistent pressure so that the glue comes out in a thin, even stream (see page 70). Trace over the design with the glue and immediately sprinkle on the pink glitter. There should be a heavy coating of glitter, with no glue showing. Leave to dry overnight.

4 When the glue is dry, shake off the excess glitter on to newspaper to reveal the design.

Leaf Print

A LUSH COLLAGE of foliage and flowers has an organic mood. Shades of green conjure up an oasis of calm, and you will feel truly tranquil when wearing this top. If green's not your colour, choose another motif, such as roses or orchids on a dusky-pink shirt.

WHAT YOU NEED

- Green T-shirt
- Copyright-free colour photocopies of leaves
- Scissors
- Plain paper
- Glue

HOW TO DO IT

1 Cut out the leaf and flower shapes. Place the T-shirt on a flat work surface and place the white paper over it. Arrange the shapes on the paper until you are pleased with the design and their position on the T-shirt, then glue them in place. Make a colour photocopy of the paper with the leaves and flowers in place.

2 Take the photocopy of the finished design to a copy shop or T-shirt-printing shop that offers colour transfers and ask for the design to be transfer printed directly on to the T-shirt in your chosen position.

Glitter-heart Pockets

DRAW ATTENTION TO YOUR DERRIERE with these sparkly hearts. Almost any other motif would work – think Evisu jeans for an abstract design, or use glittering stars. For a more suggestive look, substitute right and left hands for the hearts and work them in a larger size on the back of a pocketless skirt.

WHAT YOU NEED

- Newspaper
- Denim skirt
- Stencil card, tracing paper, pencil, cutting mat and craft knife, or a pre-cut heart stencil
- Tape measure or ruler
- Masking tape
- Stencil brush
- Strong fabric glue for glitter
- Fine washable blue glitter

HOW TO DO IT

1 Cover a flat work surface with newspaper. Place the skirt, front facing down, on the work surface and smooth it so the fabric is taut.

2 If you are cutting your own stencil, draw a heart on to the stencil card (see page 72). Alternatively, cut out a paper heart and trace around it on to the stencil card. Place the stencil card on a cutting mat and cut out the heart with a craft knife to make the stencil.

3 Centre the heart stencil on one of the back pockets. Measure to ensure that it is centred and straight, then secure it in place at each corner with masking tape.

4 Using the stencil brush, dab the fabric glue over the heart area. Immediately sprinkle on the blue glitter. There should be a heavy coating of glitter, without any glue showing through. Remove the masking tape and carefully lift off the stencil.

5 Repeat steps 3 and 4 on the other pocket and wash the stencil brush. Leave to dry for a few hours, preferably overnight, then shake off the excess glitter on to newspaper to reveal the hearts.

Silver Leopard

WHAT YOU NEED
- Pale pink cotton sweatshirt
- Cardboard
- Pre-cut leopard-print stencil
- Masking tape
- 'Invisible' or 'fade-away' pen fabric marker
- Fine-tipped artists' brush
- Transfer-foil glue
- Silver transfer foil
- Plain paper
- Iron and ironing board

THIS MUST-HAVE SWEATSHIRT has that key retro shape and the metallic silver offers a high-glam version of leopardskin. Dress it street-gang and tough with a jean skirt or hipsters and a dangling chain belt, or go for the girly look by mixing it with a sugar-almond or candy-stripe skirt.

HOW TO DO IT

1 Place the sweatshirt, front facing up, on a flat work surface. Insert a piece of cardboard measuring the width and length of the shirt to separate back and front.

2 Position the stencil over the sweatshirt, making sure that the fabric is smooth. Secure the stencil to the work surface at each corner with masking tape.

3 Working on one section at a time, use a fine-tipped paintbrush to apply glue into each shape through the stencil. Do not decorate the sleeves or the band around the bottom of the sweatshirt. Remove the tape and lift off the stencil.

4 Leave the glue to dry for the recommended time, usually four to eight hours, until the glue is clear.

5 Following the manufacturer's instructions, place the silver transfer foil, foil facing up, over the glue and smooth down. Fix the foil in position by placing plain paper over the foil and pressing with a hot iron (see page 70). Remove the paper; the foil will stick only to the glued sections.

Pink
Zebra Print

MAKE IT INTO THE A-LIST with this cool zebra-print top that will transform you from working girl to lounge lizard. Pink animal-skin prints regularly prowl down the catwalk, so you will be up there with the best. You need to be a dab hand with pen and scissors to draw and cut out the stencil, but you could photocopy a design and use it as a basis for creating your own.

WHAT YOU NEED

- Newspaper or an old sheet or fabric remnant
- Masking tape
- Camel-coloured wool vest (tank) top
- Cardboard
- Plain paper
- Pen or pencil
- Scissors
- Screen-printing screen
- Squeegee or long piece of cardboard
- Pink screen-printing ink, compatible with wool (oil-based)

SHOW TO DO IT

1 Cover a flat work surface with newspaper or an old sheet, securing it to the surface with masking tape. Place the vest (tank) top, front facing up, on the surface. Insert a piece of cardboard inside to separate back and front.

2 Draw a zebraskin design on to a piece of plain paper that measures a little larger than the top. First draw around the outline of the top so that you have a guideline for the outline of the design. Draw in ribbing or seam finishes, such as those around the arms or neckline, which you do not want to print. Then draw on the zebra stripes and patterns. If you want the edges to bleed off the sides of the top, extend the drawing outside the outline. To make cutting out the design easier, shade in the areas you want to print with a felt-tip pen or pencil. Cut out the blackened-in areas with scissors to make the zebraskin stencil.

3 Position the paper stencil over the front of the top, aligning it with your drawn marks, and secure it in place with masking tape. Make sure that the top is smooth and straight and the stencil is positioned as you like.

Any areas you do not want to print should be covered with plain paper. Place the screen-printing screen on top of the stencil.

4 Following the screen-printing instructions, pour the pink printing ink along the top end of the screen.

5 Using the squeegee or a piece of cardboard, and holding the screen down firmly with one hand, scrape the ink from end to end to print the design on to the top, using an even, firm action. Dab the squeegee or cardboard to remove excess ink, and repeat to print over the design twice (see page 71).

6 Carefully remove the screen and the paper. Discard the paper and immediately wash the screen and squeegee. Allow the ink to dry for the recommended time. When it is dry, fix the printed design according to the screen-printing instructions.

2

Dyeing & Bleaching

Learning to add colour to and take it from fabric equips you to achieve a huge range of effects and opens up a whole world of textile design. A word of warning: whether you are tie-dyeing or bleaching, you need to protect surfaces and your skin. Once you have flicked bleach on to a garment, or dyed a white T-shirt pink, there will be no turning back. If nervous, experiment on a fabric scrap first.

Vintage Lace with a **Lemon** Twist

GET THE LA VIBE with this neon mix of scorching yellow under brightest turquoise. Take joy in the unexpected: other hot colour combos that also work well are pink and turquoise, orange and yellow, or lime and cranberry. Think Day-Glo cocktails under palm trees by the beach, sweltering heat and an upfront, sassy attitude.

WHAT YOU NEED

· Old remnants of cotton lace and lace trim
· Embroidery scissors
· Turquoise fabric hand-dye
· Salt
· Yellow sleeveless cotton v-neck top
· Turquoise sewing thread
· Pins
· Cardboard
· Sewing needle

HOW TO DO IT

1 Make sure the lace is clean, dry and free of stains. Any damaged or marked areas can be simply cut away.

2 Following the dye manufacturer's instructions, dye the lace by hand in a plastic tub or basin. (Using a machine-dye and a washing machine may damage and unravel the lace.) You will need to use a quantity of salt, depending on the weight of the lace. After the specified time, rinse the lace pieces well and air-dry them.

3 When the lace is dry, place the top on a flat work surface and arrange the pieces on the front. Here a wide band of lace trim runs diagonally across the top, with another band running along the opposite top corner to complete the v-neck. An open laceworked piece has been combined with tighter-worked lace. A narrower band of trim completes the bottom border. A lace rose was placed on the point of the 'v'. When you are happy with the result, pin the pieces in place.

4 Insert a piece of card inside the top to separate back and front, then, using the turquoise thread, hand-sew each piece in position using tiny, even stitches. To clean the top, wash it carefully in cold water, rinsing constantly, so that the dye does not run. Do not soak.

Spattered T-shirt

Have a brush with authority. An olive-green T-shirt daubed and spattered with bleach and paint says you are an artist with attitude. In the manner of Jackson Pollock, gesture and action are called for in creating this abstract design. So experiment with bold splashes of bleach broken by intricate archipelagos of paint dribbling to produce your own highly individualistic work of art.

WHAT YOU NEED
· Newspaper
· Olive-green T-shirt
· 2 pieces of cardboard
· Rubber gloves
· Bleach
· Dark green fabric paint
· Paintbrushes in various sizes
· Iron and ironing board

HOW TO DO IT
1 Cover a flat work surface with newspaper. As this project involves flicking bleach, do the design outdoors if possible and wear old clothes and rubber gloves to protect your skin.

2 Make sure the T-shirt is clean and dry. Insert a large piece of cardboard inside to separate back and front, and place the T-shirt flat on the covered surface.

3 Using different sizes of paintbrush, flick bleach over the T-shirt to create patterns (see page 76). Use a quick, sharp action of the wrist and allow the bleach to soak in a little after each flicking action, as it will spread slightly. Leave the T-shirt for 20 minutes to allow the bleach to soak in. Immediately wash the brushes.

4 Machine-wash and dry the T-shirt.

5 Cover the work surface with fresh newspaper. When the T-shirt is dry, insert a new piece of cardboard inside and place it on the work surface. Using a smaller, clean paintbrush, flick dark green fabric paint over the T-shirt. Leave to dry.

6 When the paint is dry, follow the fabric paint manufacturer's instructions to fix the paint; usually this entails ironing on the reverse side of the design.

Bleached Crossed Heart

A heart motif, etched in bleach, has a stark simplicity on a plain vivid-coloured background. The heart is slightly crossed at the bottom to create a more stylized image. You could create other graffiti-like symbols or drawings, such as stick figures, noughts-and-crosses (tic-tac-toe), abstract squiggles or swirls, or brushwork a name on, as Stephen Sprouse did for Louis Vuitton.

WHAT YOU NEED
· Green top
· Cardboard
· Paper
· Scissors
· Pin
· Tape measure
· Fine-tipped artists' brush
· Bleach
· Rubber gloves

HOW TO DO IT
1 Place the top on a flat work surface and insert a piece of cardboard inside to separate back and front.

2 Cut a heart to the desired size from paper, to use as a template. Position the heart template on the front of the top with a pin, measuring to ensure that it is centred and straight.

3 Using the paintbrush and bleach, carefully hand-paint the heart around the template (see page 75). Immediately wash the brush after use.

4 When the bleach heart has appeared, after about 20 minutes, wash and dry the top.

Bleached & Dyed
Pink-Black Jeans

WITH THE CURRENT TREND to trash running at fever pitch in fashion design, try your hand at distressing and 'destroying' a pair of jeans. A key look that went from street to catwalk, bleached jeans are given a new twist here by adding colour with pink dye. The dye adds a tonal depth, while giving a splash of colour to the bleached areas, creating a cutting-edge effect that will appeal to the most die-hard trendsetter.

WHAT YOU NEED

- Newspaper
- Black denim jeans
- Bleach
- Various paintbrushes, including a 5 cm (2 in) decorating brush
- Rubber gloves
- Pink hand or machine dye
- Salt, or other recommended fixative
- Plastic bucket (if dyeing by hand)

HOW TO DO IT

1 As this project involves painting with bleach, work outdoors if possible, and wear old clothes and rubber gloves to protect your skin. Cover a flat work surface with newspaper and place the jeans on it, front facing up.

2 Paint and dribble the bleach over the jeans to create abstract patterns (see page 75). Here deep splashes were made at the hem, with finer sprays and flicks at the top. When the bleach has been absorbed, after about 40 minutes, turn the jeans over and repeat on the back.

3 When all the bleached design has developed, thoroughly wash the jeans, but do not dry them.

4 Following the dye manufacturer's instructions, dye the jeans pink, by hand or in the washing machine. You will need to use a quantity of fixative, such as salt, depending on the weight of the fabric and according to the instructions.

5 After the specified time, rinse well, then wash and air-dry the jeans.

Tie-dye
or Die

TAKE A LONG LOOK BACK with this classic tie-dye treatment – a throwback to the 1970s made contemporary. Think Venice Beach skateboarder or Malibu surfer for this laid-back casual look. The size of circles you make depends on how much fabric you gather in bunches; if you want to make circles within circles, tie an extra elastic band around the top of each bunch. The pale blue colour is subtle and soft, but for more visual punch, dye the T-shirt bright purple or orange.

WHAT YOU NEED
· White or cream T-shirt
· Pale blue hand or machine dye
· Salt, or other recommended fixative
· 5 mm (¼ in) wide elastic bands
· Plastic bucket (if dyeing by hand)
· Rubber gloves

HOW TO DO IT
1 Pre-wash the T-shirt according to the label's instructions, but do not dry.

2 While the T-shirt is still damp, tie two elastic bands at even intervals on each sleeve (see page 74). Pinch up a little fabric at the front of the T-shirt and attach an elastic band about 5 cm (2 in) from the top of the bunch. The further away from the top you attach the elastic, the larger the circle will be. Continue tying bunches of fabric on the front and back of the T-shirt.

3 Following the dye manufacturer's instructions, dye the shirt by hand in a plastic bucket or in the washing machine. You will need to use a quantity of fixative, such as salt, depending on the weight of the fabric and according to the instructions.

4 After the specified time, rinse the T-shirt well several times, then remove the elastic bands to reveal the pattern. Wash, dry and press the T-shirt.

Red & Pink
Tie-dye shirt

AN EDGING OF TWINKLING pink sequins glows against a subtle striped background, created from muted bands of pink and red dye. Red is an enduring fashion classic, and, being more vibrant and harder-edged than shades of pink, it is a fabulous colour to bestow full-on sexiness for a vampish look, or to team eye-catchingly with jeans.

WHAT YOU NEED

- White cotton thermal shirt
- Red hand dye
- Pink hand dye
- Salt, or other recommended fixative
- 2 plastic buckets
- Rubber gloves
- 5mm (¼ in) wide elastic bands
- Tape measure
- Pink sequin trim
- Pins
- Scissors
- Pink sewing thread
- Sewing needle

HOW TO DO IT

1 Pre-wash the thermal shirt according to the label's instructions, but do not dry. Then, following the dye manufacturer's instructions, prepare the red dye and pink dye with the fixative in separate buckets.

2 While the shirt is still damp, tie elastic bands around the body (but not the sleeves) at varying intervals (see page 74). If you want the stripes to be even, measure the intervals at which you tie the bands to make sure they are all the same measurement apart.

3 First dye the thermal shirt in the red dye, leaving it to soak for the recommended time. Remove from the dye bath, rinse well and remove the elastic bands.

4 Now dye the shirt in the pink dye, leaving it to soak for the recommended time. Remove from the dye bath and rinse well. Wash, dry and press the shirt.

5 Measure the circumference of the neckline and cut a length of sequin trim to size, adding 1 cm (½ in).

6 Pin the sequin trim to the neckline, overlapping the short ends neatly at a side shoulder seam to join. Hand-sew in place using a running stitch and the pink thread, following the central machined stitching in the trim.

Black-Spot T-shirt

A SIMPLE BLACK-AND-WHITE spotted shirt is dyed and embellished with a bow to match a pair of shoes. The pretty scoop-neck top would look ladylike and grown-up when teamed with a black pencil or pleated skirt. Alternatively, take a tip from Chloe Sevigny and think outside the box, perhaps teaming the top with slouchy pinstripe hipsters or a frilly vintage skirt.

WHAT YOU NEED

- White cotton shirt with black spots
- Pale blue hand or machine dye
- Salt, or other recommended fixative
- Plastic bucket (if dyeing by hand)
- Rubber gloves
- 5 mm (¼ in) wide black velvet ribbon, about 20 cm (8 in) long
- Black sewing thread
- Sewing needle

HOW TO DO IT

1 Pre-wash the shirt according to the label's instructions. Then, following the dye manufacturer's instructions, dye the shirt by hand in a plastic bucket or in the washing machine. You will need to use a quantity of fixative, such as salt, depending on the weight of the fabric and according to the instructions.

2 After the specified time, rinse well several times, then wash, dry and press the shirt.

3 Tie the black velvet ribbon in a bow. Hand-sew the bow to the centre front of the shirt, using a slip stitch (see page 78) and the black thread.

Tip

For a more art-student look, use the spot idea on a denim skirt or jeans. The spots can be 'broken up' by painting straight or curved lines across them using the bleach and a fine artists' brush.

Velvet
Spotty Skirt

CLEMENTS RIBEIRO DOESN'T HAVE a monopoly on spots. Here super-sized spots are first created with bleach, then dyed to create a graphic effect that is fresh, fun and far removed from demure polka dots. This exuberant design needs to be worn with panache, perhaps by pairing it with brightly coloured fishnets or ankle socks and vertiginous heels.

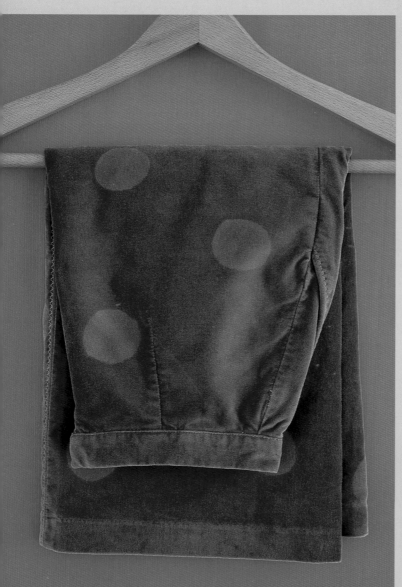

WHAT YOU NEED

- Newspaper
- Beige or neutral-coloured velvet skirt
- Cardboard
- Bleach
- Paintbrush
- Rubber gloves
- Compasses, pen, cardboard and scissors or craft knife
- Turquoise dye
- Salt, or other recommended fixative
- Plastic bucket

HOW TO DO IT

1 Cover a flat work surface with newspaper. Make sure the skirt is clean and dry. Insert a large piece of cardboard inside to separate back and front, then place the skirt flat on the covered surface. Wear old clothes and rubber gloves to protect your skin.

2 Paint the spots freehand on the skirt with the bleach (see page 75). Alternatively, use compasses and a pen to draw a circle on to cardboard and cut out the circle to make a stencil (see page 72). Position the stencil on the skirt and paint in the circle with bleach. Here the spots were made freehand, and they vary in size.

3 When you have painted the spots on the front of the skirt, turn the skirt over and paint more spots on the back.

4 Air-dry the skirt on a washing line for about 40 minutes to allow the bleach to be absorbed.

5 When the spots are clearly revealed, thoroughly wash the skirt, but do not dry it.

6 Following the dye manufacturer's instructions, prepare a turquoise dye bath and dye the skirt by hand in a plastic bucket. You will need to use a quantity of fixative, such as salt, depending on the weight of the fabric and according to the instructions.

7 After the specified time, rinse well several times, then hand-wash and air-dry the skirt.

Dip-dyed White Tanks

CREATE THESE ROTHKO-LIKE colour blocks that bleed and blur at the edges by simply dipping white tops in coloured dye. The sharp, unexpected contrast of colour against white makes a strong artistic statement. For an even more saturated and dramatic effect, try layering colours by dyeing the top a lighter colour first, such as pink or yellow, then dip-dyeing it in a stronger colour, such as red or orange.

WHAT YOU NEED
- 2 white vest (tank) tops
- Red and purple hand dye, or colours of your choice
- Salt, or other recommended fixative
- Plastic bucket
- Rubber gloves
- Washing powder (detergent)

HOW TO DO IT

1 Pre-wash the tops according to the instructions on their labels. Then, following the dye manufacturer's instructions, prepare different-colour dye baths in separate plastic buckets. You will need to use a quantity of fixative, such as salt, depending on the weight of the fabric and according to the instructions.

2 Dip each top into the dye as far as you want the dye to go. Hold in the dye until the colour is several shades deeper than the one you want.

3 Ring out the excess dye and hand-wash only the area that has been dyed with washing powder (detergent), following the dye manufacturer's instructions. Hang up the tops to air-dry.

Candy-coloured Cardigans

Tip

Don't be afraid to go for juicy lemon, orange or lime colours, and a cardigan can be dyed to match a favourite skirt or dress in a splashy fluoro floral. The dye colour will be less saturated on the lace trim.

THESE LACE-TRIMMED CARDIGANS, one pretty in pink and the other Côte d'Azur blue, are perfect partners for summery slip dresses. Whether you are a girl-about-town or holidaying in Barbados, the lightweight cardigans will keep any chills off your shoulders.

WHAT YOU NEED

- 2 white or cream thermal cotton cardigans
- Turquoise and pink hand or machine dye
- Salt, or other recommended fixative
- 2 plastic buckets (if dyeing by hand)
- Rubber gloves
- Felt flower brooch
- Tape measure
- 15 mm (⅝ in) wide green velvet ribbon trim
- Scissors
- Sewing machine
- Pins
- Green sewing thread

HOW TO DO IT

1 Pre-wash the cardigans according to the label's instructions. Then, following the dye manufacturer's instructions, dye the cardigans by hand in separate plastic buckets or in the washing machine. You will need to use a quantity of fixative, such as salt, depending on the weight of the fabric and according to the instructions.

2 After the specified time, rinse well several times, then wash, dry and press the cardigans.

3 Pin the brooch on the upper left corner of the turquoise cardigan.

4 For the pink cardigan, attach the green velvet trim. Place the cardigan on a flat surface and measure around the circumference of the cuffs and hem. Cut three lengths of velvet ribbon to size, adding 1 cm (½ in) to each.

5 Pin the velvet trim to the edge of the cuffs, flush with the inner edge of the lace trim. Turn under one short end and overlap it on to the other at the seam to join. Pin on the length of trim for the hem in the same way, but position it 1 cm (½ in) inside the edge of the hem. Measure to ensure the velvet trim is straight.

6 Using the green thread and a straight stitch, machine-stitch each length of velvet trim in place. Work as close to the edge as possible and stitch along both long sides of the velvet.

Bleach-
splattered
Denim Skirt

Tip

Experiment with
splashes, flicks, spots, dribbles,
swirls and circles of bleach on a
denim remnant before deciding
which methods to use. Gold or silver
fabric paint or broken patches of
metallic transfer foil add cool
detailing to bleached
denim.

WHAT YOU NEED

- Newspaper
- Denim skirt
- Cardboard
- Bleach
- Rubber gloves

HOW TO DO IT

1 Cover a flat work surface with newspaper. As this project involves dribbling with bleach, do the design outdoors if possible and wear rubber gloves and old clothes to protect your skin. Place the skirt on the work surface and insert a piece of cardboard inside to separate back and front.

2 Dribble the bleach straight from the container on to the skirt to create an abstract pattern (see page 75). Here an almost linear design was created by slowly pouring thin streams of bleach over the skirt. Allow the bleach to absorb for 20 minutes. Turn the skirt over and repeat on the other side. Leave for another 20 minutes.

3 When the bleach design is fully developed, thoroughly wash and air-dry the skirt.

Studded-collar Zip-up

HOW TO DO IT

Using the neck seam of the top as a guideline, mark the points where you want to position the studs with the chalk or pen fabric marker. Here three rows of studs have been made on each side of the collar and across the back collar. Insert the studs as described in step 4 of Studded-heart Sweatshirt (opposite).

WHAT YOU NEED

- Zip-up top with a high-neck collar in thick cotton jersey or sweatshirt material
- Chalk or pen fabric marker
- Tape measure
- About 100 round metal studs

Star-studded Corduroy

STUDS ARE NOT JUST FOR DENIM: they give extra punch to this deep pink corduroy skirt. Now that studs are available in star shapes, as well as in circles and colourful gemstones, the design possibilities are endless. For a dash of Hollywood glamour, bestow unexpected stardom on ordinary trousers with this simple back-pocket detailing.

WHAT YOU NEED
- Pink corduroy skirt with back pockets
- Tape measure
- Chalk or pen fabric marker
- 12 round metal studs and 2 star studs

HOW TO DO IT

1 Place the skirt on a flat work surface, with the pockets facing up. Measure and mark the positions for the star on each pocket by measuring halfway across the top edge of the pocket and measure slightly less than halfway down the length. Make a dot at these points with the chalk or pen marker.

2 Mark the positions for the round studs. Measure halfway down one side of the pocket and make a dot just inside the seam edge with the fabric marker. Repeat on the other side-seam edge of the pocket. Make two more equally spaced marks for the other studs on each side of the star so that they make a slightly curved line up to the star in the middle.

3 Check that the marked dots are equally spaced and that the design is curved enough. Then repeat step 2 for the other pocket. Hold the skirt up to make sure that the marks on both pockets match.

4 Firmly press the star stud into the fabric at the marked position for the star (see page 73). On the reverse side, bend back the prongs with your finger or a spoon to secure the stud in place. Continue the process to insert the round studs. Repeat for the other pocket.

Star-studded White Jeans

WHAT YOU NEED
- White jeans
- Tape measure
- 'Invisible' or 'fade-away' pen fabric marker
- 20 metal star studs

HOW TO DO IT
Mark the position for the star-shaped studs along the back yoke of the jeans, making sure they are equally spaced. Insert one stud at a time, as described in step 4 above.

Kaleidoscopic Dots

WHAT YOU NEED

- Black cotton round-neck top
- Cardboard
- Chalk or pen fabric marker
- Ruler or tape measure
- Strong fabric glue
- 22-28 flat-backed gemstones in assorted colours
- Tweezers

DOTS ARE HOT, and these are sparkly to boot. The brilliance of the gemstones against a dark colour makes a light-catching kaleidoscope. They can be used to add some groove to anything from a chic black top to a pair of bootleg jeans. Horizontal rows create a simple design, while diagonal rows on only one shoulder create an asymmetrical 1980s effect.

HOW TO DO IT

1 Place the top on a flat work surface and insert a piece of cardboard to separate back and front and provide a firm surface on which to work.

2 Use a fabric marker to mark the points where you want to position the gemstones. Here there are four diagonal rows of increasing numbers of gemstones across the right shoulder of the top. To do this, start with the top row and marks dots for four equally spaced gemstones. Continue with the other rows, measuring to make sure the rows are equally spaced and using the row before as a guide for positioning the gemstones.

3 Dab small amounts of glue on to several of the marks at a time and stick on the gemstones using the tweezers (see page 73). Alternate the colours so the same colours are not next to, or above or below, each other.

4 Once all the gemstones are attached, leave the top on the flat work surface overnight to dry.

Mosaic
Gemstone Jeans

WHAT YOU NEED

- Denim jeans
- Chalk or pen fabric marker
- Tape measure
- Strong fabric glue
- 80 large oval, round and square flat-backed gemstones in assorted colours
- Tweezers

HOW TO DO IT

Working on the front of the jeans first, mark the positions for two rows of gemstones on the hem of both trouser legs. Make sure that the rows are straight and equally spaced from the hem. Work the bottom row first, positioning the gemstones as described in step 3 above, and varying the shapes. Glue on the second row and leave to dry before turning the jeans over and repeating on the back.

4

Accessories

Whether it is a bag, belt or hairclip, an accessory can change the look of an outfit, and is guaranteed to grab attention. How satisfying when you can say that it is one of your own creations! Most of the techniques used in the previous chapters can be applied to accessories. Bleach and stud denim bags, or insert gemstones into a striped mesh tote. Hats, too, are endlessly transformable.

Corsage
Choker

THIS SEXY BLACK-AND-RED CHOKER lends an air of mystery and haunting beauty to a look. For a different mood, though, think frou-frou 1950s proms with pale orchids or frilly flowers in delicate pastel shades of lilac, pink or lemon meringue. Whatever colours you choose, keep other accessories to the minimum. The flower will be your focal point, so avoid hair accessories and anything but the simplest earrings. Hair swept off the face and neck also enhances the style.

WHAT YOU NEED
- Tape measure
- Scissors
- 3.5 cm (1⅓ in) wide black velvet ribbon
- Sew-on Velcro
- Black sewing thread
- Sewing needle
- Red fabric flower (or another colour of your choice)

HOW TO DO IT
1 Measure around your neck with a tape measure and add 4 cm (1½ in) to the final measurement. Cut a length of velvet ribbon to size. Fold over and press each short end by 1 cm (½ in).

2 Cut a short piece of Velcro, slightly less than the width of the ribbon and about 1 cm (½ in) long.

3 Velcro has two sides: the hook side and the loop side. Hand-sew or machine-stitch the hook side to one end of the velvet ribbon, on the right side. Check the fit to make sure the ends will overlap neatly before sewing the loop side to the other end, but on the reverse side of the ribbon. The loop side of Velcro should overlap the hook side.

4 Fold the ribbon in half lengthways to find the centre. Hand-sew the flower on to the centre front at this point, using tiny stitches to secure. Alternatively, and especially if the flower is large, sew the flower on to one side of the velvet ribbon to sit just under the jawline.

Sage Corsage on Zebra Print

A SAGE-COLOURED FLOWER softens the striking impact of this zebra-print top. While almost any accent colour – scarlet, hot pink, orange, turquoise – looks good with black and white, try using softer hues against this strong pattern for a more subtle effect. Teal, lilac, peach, sugar pink or baby blue will all work well. Don't worry about the colour being lost against the background – pretty flowers are always noticeable! You can use enormous camellias, full-blown roses or even a tiny cluster of pansies grouped together. For that *Sex and the City* look, pin a gigantic flower head on the shoulder of a slinky one-strap top.

WHAT YOU NEED

· Sage-green paper or fabric flower
· Brooch pin
· Clear 'invisible' thread and sewing needle, or strong contact glue
· Zebra-print top

HOW TO DO IT

1 Hand-sew a brooch pin on to the reverse of the flower. To make the first knot, run the thread through the pin and into the flower, leaving a little extra thread hanging. Knot the thread tightly to the hanging end, and then continue to sew, wrapping the thread around the brooch pin as you work along the length. Repeat the knot at the opposite end.

2 Alternatively, attach the flower to the pin back with a strong contact glue and allow to dry.

3 Place the top on a flat work surface and pin the corsage on the upper left side. Depending on the type of top, you can also pin it at the décolletage, or at the waist. And try one on handbags, belts, lapels, hats and scarves - even on an ankle strap of your favourite sandals (only do one, though - two is overkill).

Stripy Scarf with Appliqué Handbag

STRIPES CONTINUE TO BE A BIG TREND, appearing on the catwalk in all guises. A jolly striped scarf trimmed with fun, whimsical motifs will bring out the child in you. Try to find a scarf in as many colours as possible – you can then wear it with everything you own! If you are not so keen on the handbag idea, try making a colourful teapot, farm animal or even a little person with yarn hair who looks exactly like you to sew on the scarf.

WHAT YOU NEED

- Ready-made scarf in striped felted wool, measuring 100 x 22 cm (39 x 8½ in)
- 2 26 cm (10 in) lengths pink pom-pom trim
- Scissors
- Pins
- Sewing needle
- Beading needle
- Pink, turquoise and yellow sewing threads
- Scraps of pale blue thick felt
- Scrap of turquoise craft felt
- Fabric glue
- Short length pink sequin trim
- Button
- 9 round pink beads
- 2 turquoise glass bugle beads
- 4 cm (1½ in) pink cord
- 9 cm (3½ in) orange metallic cord

HOW TO DO IT

1 Along each short edge of the scarf, pin on the pom-pom trim, so the pom-poms hang over the edge. Turn under the raw edges on each side to align neatly with the edge of the scarf. Hand-sew in place, using a running stitch and pink thread.

2 Make the handbag. From the blue felt, cut out a shape measuring 6 cm (2¼ in) in height, 4 cm (1½ in) in width at the top and 7 cm (2¾ in) at the bottom.

3 Cut out two curved pieces for the flap, 4 cm (1½ in) in width – one in pale blue felt and the other in turquoise felt. Trim the blue piece so it is about 5 mm (¼ in) smaller along the curve. Glue the blue piece on top of the turquoise piece with the fabric glue and allow to dry.

4 Pin the sequin trim along the curve of the flap, next to the turquoise edge. Hand-sew in place with pink thread.

5 Using the yellow thread, sew the button on the centre bottom edge of the flap. Using yellow thread and a beading needle, sew the pink beads all over the front of the flap, using two stitches per bead and knotting securely. Sew a bugle bead at both corners of the flap.

6 Glue the flap on top of the handbag with the fabric glue and leave to dry. Glue or stitch the length of pink cord along the top edge of the flap.

7 To make the handle, stitch the ends of the orange cord on the back of the handbag at each outermost side, using an overhand stitch (see page 78).

8 Hand-sew the handbag to the scarf, using a decorative stitch like blanket stitch (see page 78) around the edge.

Sequinned
Flower Hat

Transform a simple woolly hat into something reminiscent of a 1920s flapper. Certain to lift spirits, it will add a flash of glamour among all the dull neutral tones worn by others in the depths of winter. This plum colour will look great on blondes and brunettes alike. A long, gently curving motif is best, as it gives a 'sweep' of decoration. Don't choose a design that is too small or geometric in shape – it needs to have some curves.

WHAT YOU NEED
- Burgundy wool hat
- Ready-made burgundy sequin floral motif
- Burgundy sewing thread
- Sewing needle

HOW TO DO IT

1 Pin the ready-made sequin motif in place on the hat. Try the hat on to check whether the positioning is correct. The motif will look best when it frames the face on one side.

2 Hand-sew the motif in place using a slip stitch (see page 78). To anchor the knot, sew a few stitches into the wool and tie the ends in a knot before sewing and when finishing off. Take care to work slowly and evenly so that the hat does not stretch out of shape while you are decorating it.

Pink Net
and PVC Bag

TAKE THE EDGE OFF high-sheen PVC with a frill of colourful spotted net and transform an inexpensive bag into an original one-of-a-kind. The contrast of textures and colours works to create a bag that is hardcore, yet undeniably feminine. For a night out, pair it with knee-high black patent-leather boots and exude a devil-may-care attitude that hints at serious seductive powers.

WHAT YOU NEED

- Black PVC bag
- Tape measure
- Pink-spotted netting
- Scissors
- Pins
- Sewing machine
- Pink and black threads
- 15 mm ($\frac{5}{8}$ in) wide black satin ribbon

HOW TO DO IT

1 Measure the circumference of the rim of the black bag. Cut a length of pink net three times this measurement. Decide on the depth of the frill and cut it to size. Here an 8 cm (3¼ in) deep frill has been used on a 32 x 24 cm (12 ½ x 9½ in) bag.

2 Fold and pin under the short ends of the net. Fold even, equally spaced pleats along the length of the net, pinning them in place (see page 76). Check the length by holding the net along the rim. Adjust the pleats and trim the net, if necessary, to achieve the correct length.

3 Begin to machine-stitch the net on to the bag. Line the net up with one side seam and about 1 cm (½ in) below the rim. Holding the net in your hand, machine-stitch the net to the bag. Work all the entire way around the rim, removing the pins as you go.

4 Cut a length of black ribbon measuring 2.5 cm (1 in) more than the circumference of the rim. Pin it to the edge of the bag to cover the pink net seam, turning under the short raw edge at the join. Using black thread, machine-stitch along both long sides to finish.

Star-studded Belt

WHY SPEND A FORTUNE on a Marc by Marc Jacobs rainbow belt when you can decorate a simple webbed belt with colourful studs? Orange is a key vibrant colour, one massively popular in the 1970s. The studs can be worked evenly in a row or at different heights for a more visually interesting effect. For example, keep all the studs at the same level except for coloured gemstone studs, or smaller studs, which 'break out' of line. For a wild zing of colour, to jazz up a dark denim skirt or jeans, nothing could be hipper.

WHAT YOU NEED
- Orange webbed belt
- Selection of gemstone and metal studs in assorted colours
- Chalk or pen fabric marker

1 On a flat work surface, arrange the studs in a row, moving them about to alternate shapes and colours.

2 When you have decided on the positions for them, use the fabric marker to mark out dots on the belt where you will insert the studs. Make sure the dots are evenly spaced, but remember that some of the studs are bigger than others, so you will need to allow more space around them.

3 Following the manufacturer's instructions, press the first stud firmly into the fabric at the mark (see page 76). On the reverse side, bend back the prongs with your finger or a metal spoon to secure the stud.

4 For gemstone studs, push the pronged piece through the belt from the reverse side at the marked position. Insert the stone into the centre and bend the prongs around the stone with a finger or a metal spoon to secure it.

5 Continue steps 3 and 4, as necessary, to insert all the gemstone and metal studs.

TAKE A SIMPLE BERET, ET VOILA C'EST TRES CHIC

Glitzy Beret

WHO NEEDS PARIS? Berets look chic and stylish wherever you go. Their simple shape offers endless possibilities when it comes to customizing. You could try a post-Punk design with red sequins, safety pins and tiny badges on a black beret, or go for the urban military look with gold cord and brass buttons on Army green.

WHAT YOU NEED

- Moss-green wool beret
- Assorted sequins in different shapes and colours
- Chalk or pen fabric marker (optional)
- Clear 'invisible' thread
- Beading needle

HOW TO DO IT

1 Place your sequins on a flat work surface and move them about to decide which ones work well together. Use sequins in a mixture of different shapes and colours, as here, or keep to a same-colour theme but with sequins in all sort of shapes. Keep for another project the ones that don't work with the others.

2 If desired, mark a dot with the fabric marker at the points where you want to position each sequin .

3 Hand-sew the sequins all over the beret. To do this, first make a knot in the invisible thread, and then bring the needle through to the right side of the beret. Secure each sequin with a few stitches. For sequins with cental holes, make two stitches at opposite edges of the sequin.

Feather & Velvetea
Slippers

L OW-HEELED PINK SATIN slippers with leopard print lining look extra-exotic when trimmed with turquoise feathers. This would look equally good on a pair of high-heels as a take on the marabou mule. Perfect for padding about your bedroom or for entertaining at home, these slippers should be seen and admired.

HOW TO DO IT

1 Measure the width of the front of the slipper where you want to attach the trim. Cut two strips of feather trim to size. Cut two strips of velvet ribbon to size, adding 1 cm (½in) to each.

2 Using the hot-glue gun, apply the glue along the rim of one slipper and immediately stick one piece of the feather trim in place. Hold for a few seconds, then leave to dry. Repeat with the other slipper.

3 Turn under and glue both short ends of each velvet ribbon by ½ cm (¼in). When dry, glue the velvet trim on to the edge of each slipper, using the glue gun. Hold for a few seconds, then allow to dry.

4 To attach the gems, dab dots of glue, equally spaced, on the velvet ribbon (see page 73). Glue 10-12 gems on each shoe.

WHAT YOU NEED
- Low-heeled fabric slippers
- Tape measure
- Turquoise feather trim
- Narrow lime velvet ribbon
- Scissors
- Hot-glue gun (see page 77)
- 20-24 turquoise flat-backed gemstones

Tropical
Flower Flip-flops

P INK SILK FLIP-FLOPS with black velvet thongs are used here for an exotic tropical look, but you could also decorate plain rubber flip-flops in the same way. Choose large plastic flowers in colours that complement your shoes. Whether you are wearing these for a summer garden party, to a picnic in the park or simply to the beach, they will lend a South Pacific note to the occasion. Team them with a sarong, tiny T-shirt and vividly painted toenails.

WHAT YOU NEED
- Silk-and-velvet or plastic flip-flops
- 2 plastic flowers
- Super-glue or strong contact glue for plastics

HOW TO DO IT

1 Make sure the flip-flops are clean and dry.

2 Glue a flower to the front of the thong of each flip-flop. To do this, coat both sides to be adhered, press firmly together so that the glue can bond, then leave to dry. Follow the manufacturer's instructions for the glue. Some contact glues require you to mix two solvents, or to wait for a designated time before sticking the surfaces together.

Glitter Swirl Belt

THERE IS NO NEED TO GO ALL-OUT with military style if it is not your thing - just take a token accessory, like this Army-style webbed belt, and add a bit of girly glamour with glitter. Special fabric glitter, most often used for T-shirt decoration, is available from craft shops, specialist sewing shops, and the craft departments of large stores. As a variation on this design, choose a glitter in the same colour as the belt, but highlight the pattern with gold or silver glitter. Because glitter can be tricky and a little unwieldy, use it with an abstract motif; don't make the design too fussy or ornate. Try using script writing if your belt is wide enough - a simple word, like babe or foxy, looks good in curvy letters on the back of the belt.

WHAT YOU NEED

· Newspaper
· Teal-blue webbed belt
· Cardboard or masking tape
· Chalk or pen fabric marker (optional)
· Fabric glue
· Fine washable purple fabric glitter

1 Place newspaper on a work surface to help you clean up any spilled glitter later on. Either pin the belt to a length of cardboard or stick the ends to the work surface with masking tape so that the belt does not move while you work.

2 Decide on the pattern you want to create. If you are unsure of working freehand, draw out your design on paper to the correct dimensions, then copy it on to the belt, using a chalk or pen fabric marker.

3 Practise squeezing out the fabric glue before you start; apply consistent pressure so that the glue comes out in a thin, even stream. Squeeze the fabric glue on to the belt to create the swirly pattern (see page 70).

4 Sprinkle the purple glitter over the glue. There should be a heavy coating, without any glue showing through. Leave overnight to dry.

5 When it is dry, carefully shake off the excess glitter.

Gold-splattered Denim Bag

THIS TAKE ON GLITZY GOLD uses Jackson Pollock-inspired splatters on a simple denim bag. If you really like this effect, try it on jeans (the colour works best against a dark denim background). You could try other colours, too, but use only one colour of a metallic paint - you don't want to look as if you have been decorating your home. Practise first on paper if you are unsure of the effect you want to achieve. The long handle of the paintbrush will make the flicking technique easier to master.

WHAT YOU NEED

· Newspaper
· Plain dark denim bag
· Gold fabric paint
· 1 cm (½ in) wide artists' paintbrush, with a 25 cm (10 in) handle

HOW TO DO IT

1 Cover a large flat work surface with old newspapers. Place the denim bag, front facing up, on the newspaper.

2 Dip the paintbrush into the gold paint and flick it over the bag in various directions, using a quick wrist action (see page 76). When you have applied enough splatters, leave the bag to dry.

3 When the paint is dry, turn the bag over and apply the paint on the other side. Allow to dry.

Sequin Sneakers

WHAT YOU NEED
· Red canvas sneakers
· Super-glue
· About 90 silver diamantés
· Tweezers
· 4 pink flat-backed
  star gemstones

MAKE THOSE SNEAKERS SPARKLE

Everybody's been getting into the trend for customizing their Converses, so get out your favourite pair and give them a new lease of life. Merge comfort and style with these rhinestone-encrusted sneakers – wearing them with bare legs and a short skirt is a current catwalk look. For a variation on this theme, bead sections of the shoe, or make a patchwork of logos or logoed ribbons (the type that come tied to your designer shopping bag) for that 'I can't live without my labels' look.

HOW TO DO IT

1 Apply the glue in a thin stream along the side seams on one of the sneakers. Then, using a pair of tweezers, position the diamantés on the glue, working along the lines (see page 73). Glue them on one at a time and as close together as possible. Allow to dry.

2 When the glue is dry, repeat step 1 to attach the diamanté gems on the other side of the shoe. Repeat the process for the other sneaker.

3 To finish, glue a star gemstone to both sides of each sneaker. Allow to dry.

Feather Hairclips

ONCE THE UBIQUITOUS TRIM for hats, brooches and hair accessories, feathers are now enjoying a renaissance. Clipped into nape-of-neck chignons or just holding back hair above the ear, their gentle fringing effect frames the face and provides a contrast of texture to sleek shiny hair. You could try peacock feathers for the show-off in you, ostrich plumes for some movie-star glamour, Native American-inspired browns and golds, or the multipatterned feathers shown here.

HOW TO DO IT

1 Arrange the feathers to make an attractive bouquet. Use longer, thinner feathers underneath shorter, wider ones. Trim the quills and tie the ends with a short length of wire or adhesive tape.

2 Cut a length of velvet ribbon to secure the feathers. Apply fabric glue on to the reverse side of the ribbon. Remove the wire or tape from the quill ends and wrap the velvet around the ends of the feather bouquet, overlapping the ends on the underside.

3 Apply four drops of glue on to the velvet ribbon and stick on the gemstones, pressing in place to ensure they adhere. Allow to dry.

4 Open out the hairclip. Using a super-glue or a hot-glue gun (see page 77), apply a thin stream of glue along the top of the clip. Line up the ribbon end of the feathers with the top end of the clip where it fastens, and stick it in place. If you are using a hot-glue gun, the feathers will stick immediately to the clip; if using a super glue, you will need to hold the clip and feathers together until the glue begins to harden.

5 Leave the clip to dry overnight before wearing it.

How-to Techniques

BOTH THE TECHNIQUES shown here use a freehand method of painting a design in glue, though one is completed in glitter and the other in iron-on transfer foil. Transfer foils enable a multitude of effects, from a scattering of small dots to a big foil heart, star or number. Because the foil is available in different colours, you have many more choices than simply gold or silver – try multicoloured spots or layer self-colours, such as a metallic blue against a b lue fabric, to enhance the contrast of textures.

GLUEING GLITTER

1 Squeeze the glue over the fabric in a thin, even stream to create an abstract pattern. Use a glue that is compatible with the glitter, and the same brand.

2 While the glue is still wet, sprinkle on a generous amount of fine machine-washable glitter. Make sure that no glue shows through.

3 Leave the glue to dry for several hours, preferably overnight. When it is dry, shake off the excess glitter on to paper to reveal the design. The surplus glitter can be reused.

PRINTING FOIL

1 Paint the design freehand on to the fabric using a fabric glue that is compatible with and the same brand as the transfer foil. Leave for four to eight hours, until the glue is clear.

2 Place the transfer foil, foil facing up, over the glued area and smooth down. Fix the foil by placing plain paper on top and ironing over the design with smooth strokes.

3 Let the design cool for a few minutes, then peel off the paper to reveal the design. The foil will stick only to the glued area.

How-to Techniques

PRINTING TECHNIQUES enable a uniformity of design. Rubber stamping is one of the easiest methods for printing a repeat motif, and it can be used on soft furnishings as well as clothing. Though screen printing seems tricky, once you master it you can print many copies of a design; it is a good way to print T-shirts (as well as flyers or posters) for a club or organization.

SCREEN PRINTING

1 Draw the shape you want to print on to a piece of plain paper and cut it out to make a stencil. Position the stencil in place on the garment. Place the screen on top.

2 Pour screen-printing paint in a line along the top end of the screen to the width of the design and about 5 cm (2 in) above the stencil, following the paint instructions.

3 Holding the squeegee at a 45-degree angle, scrape the paint from end to end. Dab the squeegee to remove excess paint, add more paint if needed, and repeat.

4 Carefully lift off the screen and remove the stencil. Allow the ink to dry for the recommended time. When it is dry, fix the printed design according to the instructions.

RUBBER STAMPING

1 Pour or squeeze a small amount of the paint on to a flat plate or tile. Roll the foam roller in the paint. Roll the roller evenly over the rubber stamp to transfer the paint.

2 Press the stamp down on to the fabric. Do not coat the stamp with too much paint or the detail will be lost; do not use too little paint, or the design will be faint.

How-to Techniques

STENCILS ARE NECESSARY for many decorative crafts, but once made, they can be reused for different media if cleaned and stored properly. To make a stencil, use a pen or marker to draw around a template, or draw an image freehand, on to a piece of stencil card, leaving a margin of 7 cm (2 ¾ in) around the edge. If the design is highly detailed, colour in the areas to be cut out with a black felt-tip pen. Place the stencil card on a cutting mat and cut out the shape, using a craft knife.

STENCILLING WITH GLITTER

1 Position the stencil on the garment and secure it in place with masking tape at each corner. Dab the stencil brush in the fabric glitter glue and dab inside the stencil.

2 Sprinkle the machine-washable glitter over the glue while it is still wet. Allow the glue to dry for several hours, preferably overnight.

3 When it is dry, remove the masking tape, carefully lift off the stencil, and shake off the excess glitter on to paper. The extra glitter can be reused for another project.

STENCILLING WITH FABRIC PAINT

1 Position the stencil on the garment and secure it with masking tape at each corner. Dab a stencil brush in the fabric paint sparingly and dab inside the cut-out areas.

2 When the design is painted, remove the masking tape and carefully lift off the stencil so as not to smudge the paint. Allow the paint to dry for the recommended time.

How-to Techniques

STUDS AND GEMSTONES add fashionable style to jeans, jackets, handbags and T-shirts. The techniques for applying them are so easy and quick that you will have almost instant results. You can decorate a T-shirt with studs in just a few minutes' time and wear it immediately – no fuss, no waiting and no tricky materials to use. Flat-backed gemstones and diamantés in every colour under the sun can be added with just a dab of fabric glue.

INSERTING STUDS

1 Measure and mark positions for the metal studs, using a chalk or pen fabric marker. The studs look best positioned along a hem or seam and equally spaced apart.

2 Firmly press the stud into the fabric from the right side, at the desired position.

3 Turn the fabric to the reverse side and bend the prongs inward, using your thumb and fingers, a metal spoon or a screwdriver, to secure the stud in place.

ATTACHING GEMSTONES AND DIAMANTES

1 Dab a small amount of strong fabric glue on to the spots where you want to position the flat-backed gemstones or diamantés.

2 Pick up each gemstone, using a pair of tweezers, and position it on the glue. Allow to dry before moving the fabric.

How-to Techniques

Aᴌᴛʜᴏᴜɢʜ ᴛɪᴇ-ᴅʏᴇɪɴɢ is a familiar technique for most people, it is often an inexact science – however, sometimes the unexpected yields the best results. Be bold with your tying techniques if you feel the ones shown here are too simplistic, but do get to know colours and how they mix. As a general rule, dye with darker colours first, using progressively lighter dyes as you work.

BASIC TIE-DYEING

1 To create circular designs on a shirt, pinch a little fabric on a damp 100% cotton shirt and secure with an elastic band. Repeat all over the shirt. The more fabric you pinch, the larger the circle will be.

2 To create stripes, tie elastic bands at varying intervals around a damp 100% cotton shirt. If you want even stripes, measure the intervals at which you tie the bands to make sure they are all the same.

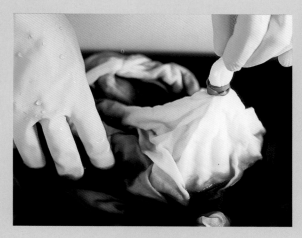

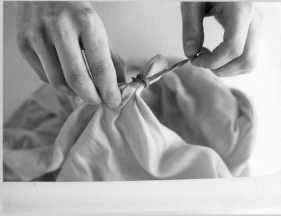

3 Prepare a dye bath according to the dye instructions. You will need to dissolve the dye and fixative in a bucket of warm water. Dip the garment into the dye and allow to soak for the recommended time.

4 Squeeze the excess dye from the garment and rinse well several times in cold water. Remove the elastic bands to reveal the design and hang the garment up to dry.

How-to Techniques

BLEACH IS A LOT MORE ADAPTABLE to painterly expression than you might think. Bold, haphazard splashes of reverse-dyed fabric are not the only option: bleaching techniques can be controlled and meticulous, too. Delicate line etchings in bleach can give clothing an intricate pictorial quality. Here are techniques for detailed work as well as for expressionistic and abstract designs.

POURING BLEACH

5 Here is one of the many colour effects that can be created using tie-dyeing techniques, as shown left.

1 To create abstract designs, simply pour liquid household bleach on the surface of fabric. Use bleach only on 100% cotton fabrics, wear rubber gloves, and protect surrounding surfaces.

PAINTING WITH BLEACH

1 Pour a small amount of liquid household bleach into a plastic bowl. Dip a paintbrush into the bleach and paint the design on to the fabric as if you were using paint.

How-to Techniques

ANY OF THE TECHNIQUES described throughout the book can be employed with accessories. If you are concerned about committing a design to an item of clothing, begin with an inexpensive belt or bag. A layering of effects works well, too; for example, embellish a bleached denim handbag with beading and flicks of metallic paint, or use glitter glue and studs on a belt.

ATTACHING NET FRILL

1 Pleat the net evenly, securing it with pins to the bag as you work. Adjust the pleats to fit the entire way around the bag, as necessary, and stitch in place using a running stitch.

FLICKING PAINT

1 Dip a long-handled artists' brush in the paint, then flick it on to the surface of the fabric, using a quick wrist action. Intersperse flicks with long dribbles of paint. Allow to dry.

ATTACHING GEMSTONE AND DIAMANTE STUDS

1 Decide on the arrangement you want for the gemstones. Mark the positions with a chalk or pen fabric marker.

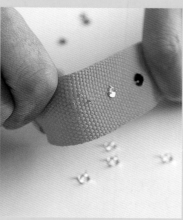

2 Firmly press the stud clasp into the fabric from the reverse side, at the desired position, until the prongs protrude from the surface.

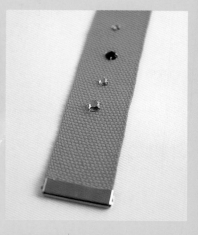

3 Place the gemstone between the prongs, then bend the prongs over the stone with your fingers or a metal spoon to secure it.

Glossary

TOOLS

BEADING NEEDLE
A fine needle for sewing on beads that have very small holes.

CARDBOARD
Cardboard is available in various thicknesses and qualities. Use thicker card for inserting inside clothes when painting, bleaching or printing to stop the paint or bleach going through to the other side of the fabric. Cardboard is also useful for hand-sewing, and as a substitute for a hoop for embroidery work to prevent stitching through to the other side of the article.

CHALK FABRIC MARKER
A chalk marker is useful for marking designs and measurements on to fabric, and it rubs or washes out. Some versions have a brush eraser at the end for removing the marks.

CRAFT KNIFE
A sharp cutting knife, such as a Stanley or X-Acto knife, should be used to cut out stencils. Alternatively use a thin-bladed scalpel, which is ideal for cutting out more intricately designed and curved shapes.

CUTTING MAT
A rubber mat that is used with a craft knife for cutting out stencils. It prevents the stencil from slipping and protects the work surface.

ELASTIC BANDS
Available in various sizes and thicknesses, the bands are used for tie-dying techniques.

EMBROIDERY HOOP
Wooden or plastic hoops that secure fabric and keep it taut for working decorative stitches.

GLUE GUN
This electrical tool enables instant glueing and will avoid the need for pressing or clamping pieces together until they are dry. To apply the glue, insert the special glue sticks, heat up the gun and press the trigger; the glue is released through the nozzle. Although the gun cannot be used on items you want to wash, it is ideal for adding gemstones, appliqués and trims to shoes and handbags or for attaching brooch pins to fake flowers.

IRON
An iron is essential for pressing clothes and ironing on transfers and heat-fusible webbing.

INVISIBLE OR FADE-AWAY FABRIC MARKER
A special felt-tip pen used for marking fabric. The marks disappear with time.

NEEDLES
Available in a variety of sizes, specific needles are used with different types and weights of thread. Use Sharps for hand-sewing, embroidery needles for stranded embroidery thread, and tapestry needles for tapestry wool or yarn.

PAINTBRUSHES
Owning a good range of different paintbrushes will enable you to create a huge variety of effects. Use large, medium and small house-decorating brushes for creating bold splashes of colour when fabric painting or bleaching. Use fine-tipped artists' brushes for detailed work and flicking paint or bleach. Always wash brushes thoroughly after use.

PINS
Use pins for temporarily securing fabrics together, pinning up a hem or pinning on trimmings prior to sewing. Coloured-head pins are easier to see and remove than dressmaker's pins.

RULER
A transparent version allows you to see what you are measuring and enables you to line up letters or numbers horizontally. Any type of ruler is helpful when centring a design or for marking straight lines on fabric.

SCISSORS
Use sharp sewing scissors for cutting fabric and trims. Use embroidery scissors for cutting threads and trimmings, or for cutting out intricate appliqués. Use craft scissors for cutting paper or card. Do not use sewing scissors for cutting paper, as over time the blades will blunt.

SCREEN-PRINTING SCREEN
This is a basic wooden frame with a nylon mesh stretched over it. Screens can be purchased in a variety of sizes from craft suppliers or art shops.

SEWING MACHINE
A sewing machine enables you to create a variety of stitches, from straight and zigzag stitches to satin stitching or monogramming. Using a machine is a speedy way to attach trims and appliqués or to hem fabric.

SLEEVE BOARD
A small narrow board that clips on to an ironing board, a sleeve board is ideal for working on small areas, such as trouser legs or sleeves.

SQUEEGEE
A rubber-edged implement used for dragging paint across a screen-printing screen. You can substitute a thick piece of cardboard.

STENCIL BRUSH
This stubby brush with short bristles is essential for dabbing paint through a stencil. Use a large size of brush, such as a 6, for large-scale designs, and a small size, such as a 4, for more detailed stencils.

STENCIL CARD
This is a professional paper made specifically for stencils. It is similar to thin cardboard, but waterproof, and it is available as plain cards for drawing on to and cutting out your own designs. Transparent stencil plastic is a useful alternative, but you will need to use an electric stencil cutter.

STENCILS
Pre-cut stencil designs are ready to use. They are usually cut out from a washable, reusable material, such as stencil card or acetate.

TAPE MEASURE
A flexible measuring tape that is essential for measuring fabric.

TWEEZERS
Use straight-edged cosmetic tweezers for picking up and positioning small gemstones.

MATERIALS

BEADS
Hundreds of different shapes, colours and textures of beads are available from craft shops, department stores or beading shops. Most of the beads used throughout the book are small round or straight glass beads.

BLEACH
This standard household fluid can be used to discolour and fade colour when it is applied on to natural fabrics and denims. Use caution when handling, as the bleach will discolour any fabric or furnishing on to which it splashes.

FABRIC DYE
Many brands and types are available; they are usually sold as either for hand-dyeing or for machine-dyeing. Refer to manufacturer's instructions before use, and make sure the dye is suitable for the fabric you are using.

FABRIC GLUE

This is a special adhesive used for glueing fabric shapes, trims or gemstones on to fabric. Always make sure the glue you use is suitable for the materials. Using the same brand as the decoration will ensure the best possible adhesion. Glues specifically for use with washable glitter and sequins, or transfer foils, are available.

FABRIC PAINT

This is a special paint that can be applied on to fabric. Once fixed, usually by ironing it on the reverse side of the design, it is fully washable. Read the manufacturer's advice for fabrics to use and fixing techniques.

FEATHER TRIM

Available in various colours and styles, feather trims are secured in a simple ribbon binding for stitching on. Often feather trims include beads or a decorative trim, and can be hand-sewn on to the right side of a garment or accessory.

FELT

This is a cloth made from pressed wool. You can buy squares of craft felt in a multitude of colours from craft or specialist sewing shops. It is easy to cut and does not fray. Felted wool is a thicker more textured fabric than craft felt and can be purchased by the metre (yard) from sewing shops.

GEMSTONE STUDS

These are metal clasps that have four prongs for holding gemstones. They are pressed through from the reverse side of the fabric and a gemstone is inserted in the prongs. The prongs are then bent over the stone to hold it in place.

GEMSTONES OR DIAMANTES

These sparkly synthetic stones can be glued in place with fabric glue or a super-glue. They can also be inserted into gemstone studs.

GLITTER FABRIC PAINT

This is a clear fabric paint containing fine glitter particles, available in a range of colours. When the paint is dry, the glitter sparkles.

MACHINE-WASHABLE GLITTER

This super-fine glitter in a range of colours can only be applied to clothing with a special fabric glue made by the same company as the glitter. Read the manufacturer's instructions for application techniques.

MACHINE-WASHABLE TRANSFER FOIL

This is a decorative foil and can only be applied with a special fabric glue made by the same company as the foil. The transfer foil is available in a range of colours. Read the manufacturer's instructions for application techniques.

METAL STUDS

These are available in silver and gold metal and in different shapes and sizes. They have four prongs, which are inserted through the right side of the fabric. The prongs are then opened out and pressed flat on the reverse side of the fabric to hold the stud in place.

PUFFA PAINT

This is a heat-reactive paint that can be applied directly to fabric to create a textural design. When the paint is dry, the design is turned reverse side out and ironed, at which point the paint magically starts to puff up. Never iron the paint directly. Read the manufacturer's instructions.

RIBBON ROSES

These can be purchased ready-made. They can also be made by wrapping a short length of narrow ribbon into a rosette and securing the shape in place with a few stitches.

RIBBONS AND TRIMMINGS

An array of textures, colours, styles, patterns and widths are available, from velvet ribbon, sequin trim and fringing to lace, rickrack and cord. Many can be machine-stitched in place, but more delicate lace and beadwork will need to be hand-sewn.

SEQUINS

Loose sequins have tiny holes that allow them to be stitched in place individually. Sequins are also available without holes, and these are glued on with strong fabric glue. Sequin trim is a decorative length of small round sequins held together with thread, which can be hand-sewn or machine-stitched in place.

SUPER-GLUE OR CONTACT GLUE

A very strong contact glue that immediately bonds materials together. Read the manufacturer's advice for materials that can be bonded and always follow the application instructions. These types of glue should not be used on clothing.

THREADS

General-purpose cotton or polyester thread is used for hand-sewing and machine-stitching. Stranded cotton embroidery thread (floss) is used for decorative stitching; usually this is available six-stranded and the strands can be separated for finer work. Tapestry wool or yarn is much thicker than embroidery thread and is often used for embroidery work on heavier woollen garments.

TRANSFER PRINT

A coloured image is photocopied on to special transfer paper, which is then positioned on a garment or fabric and transferred, using a special press. The technique requires enlisting the help of a specialist copy or T-shirt-printing shop.

SEWING STITCHES

BLANKET STITCH

This stitch is used to hem raw edges, or as decoration. Insert the needle through the fabric so that it points up to the top edge , wind the loose thread over the needle and pull it through the loop.

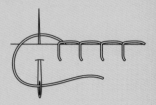

SLIP STITCH

This stitch is used to hem fabric. With the needle, sew into the folded hem fabric and catch a thread from the main fabric, spacing the stitches evenly apart.

OVERHAND

These tiny, even stitches are used to join two finished edges – for example, attaching ribbon or lace edging to a garment. Insert the needle diagonally from the back edge through to the front, picking up only one or two threads each time. Insert the needle directly behind the thread from the previous stitch and bring it out a stitch length away.

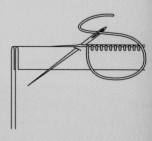

Resources

Acknowledgements

F. W. BRAMWELL & CO. LTD
Old Empress Mills
Empress Street
Colne, Lancs BB8 9HU
0123 286 0388
www.bramwellcrafts.co.uk
Glitter, foils, fabric glue and paint,
gemstones and more.

DOVER BOOKSHOP
18 Earlham St
London WC2H 9LG
020 7836 2111
www.doverbooks.co.uk
Copyright-free design books.

DYLON INTERNATIONAL LTD
Worsley Bridge Rd
London SE26 5HD
Advice line: 020 8663 4296
www.dylon.co.uk
Fabric dyes, paints and pens.

ELLS & FARRIER
20 Beak Street
London W1F 9RE
020 7629 9964
www.creativebeadcraft.co.uk
Beads, gemstones, studs and
trimmings.

THE ENGLISH STAMP
COMPANY
Worth Matravers
Dorset BH19 3JP
0192 943 9117
www.englishstamp.com
Rubber stamps and fabric paint.

HOMECRAFTS DIRECT
PO Box 38
Leicester LE1 9BU
0845 458 4532
Screen-printing equipment,
screen inks and catalogue.

JOHN LEWIS PLC
Oxford Street
London W1A 1EX
020 7629 7711
www.johnlewis.co.uk

THE STENCIL LIBRARY
Stocksfield Hall
Stocksfield
Northumberland NE43 7TN
01661 844 844
www.stencil-library.com
Stencils in all sorts of designs.

The following companies were
very helpful in lending props for
the photography shoots:

ANDREW MARTIN (wallpapers)
200 Walton Street
London SW3 2JL
020 7225 5100

CATH KIDSTON
8 Clarendon Cross
London W11 4AP
020 7221 4000
www.cathkidston.co.uk

JACQUELINE EDGE
1 Courtnell Street
London W2 5BU
020 7229 1172
www.jacquelineedge.com

MUJI
Whiteleys Shopping Centre
London W2 4YN
Mail order: 020 7792 8283
www.muji.co.jp

THE PAINT LIBRARY
5 Elystan Street
London SW3 3NT
020 7823 7755
www.paintlibrary.co.uk

PAPERCHASE
213 Tottenham Court Road
London W1T 9PS
020 7467 6200
www.paperchase.co.uk

SANDERSONS
Sanderson House
Oxford Road
Denham, Bucks UB9 4DX
www.sanderson-online.com

I would like to thank the following
designers for their customizing
contributions:
Nancy Bridgewater
Katy Hackney
Claire Kitchener
Kim Robertson
Emma Eardley

Index